Wadsworth Public Library
132 Broad Street
Wadsworth, OH 44281

JAPANESE MYTHOLOGY

Ebisu

BY GOLRIZ GOLKAR

CONTENT CONSULTANT
ADAM L. KERN, PhD
PROFESSOR OF JAPANESE LITERATURE AND VISUAL CULTURE
UNIVERSITY OF WISCONSIN–MADISON

Kids Core
An Imprint of Abdo Publishing
abdobooks.com

abdobooks.com

Published by Abdo Publishing, a division of ABDO, PO Box 398166, Minneapolis, Minnesota 55439. Copyright © 2025 by Abdo Consulting Group, Inc. International copyrights reserved in all countries. No part of this book may be reproduced in any form without written permission from the publisher. Kids Core™ is a trademark and logo of Abdo Publishing.

Printed in the United States of America, North Mankato, Minnesota.
102024
012025

THIS BOOK CONTAINS RECYCLED MATERIALS

Cover Photos: Ann Hirna/Shutterstock Images (foreground); Shutterstock Images (background)
Interior Photos: Print Collector/Hulton Archive/Getty Images, 4–5; Rodolfo Contreras/Alamy, 7; Archive PL/Alamy, 8, 28 (top); Pictures From History/CPA Media Pte Ltd/Alamy, 10, 28 (bottom); Chronicle/Alamy, 12–13; Shutterstock Images, 15, 23, 26; Universal History Archive/Universal Images Group/Getty Images, 16, 29 (top); Adb Kun/Shutterstock Images, 18; ARTGEN/Alamy, 20–21; Danita Delimont/Alamy, 25, 29 (bottom)

Editor: Christa Kelly
Series Designer: Ryan Gale

Library of Congress Control Number: 2024938398

Publisher's Cataloging-in-Publication Data

Names: Golkar, Golriz, author.
Title: Ebisu / by Golriz Golkar
Description: Minneapolis, Minnesota: ABDO Publishing, 2025 | Series: Japanese mythology | Includes online resources and index.
Identifiers: ISBN 9781098295950 (lib. bdg.) | ISBN 9798384916956 (ebook)
Subjects: LCSH: Mythology, Japanese--Juvenile literature. | Deities--Juvenile literature. | Ebisu (Japanese deity)--Juvenile literature. | Webisu (Japanese deity)--Juvenile literature. | Mythology, Asian--Juvenile literature.
Classification: DDC 398.21--dc23

CONTENTS

CHAPTER 1
The Leech Child 4

CHAPTER 2
The Seven Lucky Gods 12

CHAPTER 3
Honoring Ebisu 20

Legendary Facts 28
Glossary 30
Online Resources 31
Learn More 31
Index 32
About the Author 32

Izanagi, *left*, and Izanami, *right*, are the gods who created Japan.

CHAPTER **1**

The Leech Child

There once were two gods. Their names were Izanagi and Izanami. The gods wanted to have a child. They performed a **ritual** to create a baby. But something went wrong. When their child was born, he had no bones. He looked like a **leech**.

Izanagi and Izanami named the child Hiruko (pronounced hee-roo-koh). The name meant *leech child*.

For three years, Izanagi and Izanami waited for Hiruko to walk. Finally, they decided to abandon the boy. They put him in a boat made of reeds and cast him off to sea.

After sailing for a while, Hiruko drifted ashore. A local people called the Ainu found him. Among the people was an Ainu god named Ebisu (eh-bee-soo) Saburo. The god decided to raise the little leech boy.

Hiruko remained sick for years. But one day, he grew a skeleton and learned to walk. He took Ebisu's name to honor the god who had raised him.

The Ainu are native to northern Japan.

In Japanese, *ebisu* means "stranger" or "someone from another place."

Ebisu still had **disabilities** from his illness. He was deaf and had difficulty walking. But he was happy. He was grateful for surviving the rough seas. He decided to share his happiness and good luck with others. Today, Ebisu is the god of fishers and **merchants**. People pray to him for good luck.

What Is Japanese Mythology?

Japan is an island country off the eastern coast of Asia. Many people in Japan practice a religion called Shinto. The word *Shinto* means "way of the gods." Around 89 million people in Japan practice Shinto.

Spirits of the Sea

Some Japanese fishers used to worship sea creatures. They believed that some sea animals, such as whales and dolphins, were **incarnations** of Ebisu. They considered these animals to be spirits of the sea. Some believed that even driftwood or stones washed up on the shore might be incarnations of Ebisu.

Ebisu is sometimes called the Laughing God.

Japanese mythology is an important part of Shinto. This mythology often centers around *kami,* or "spirits." There are many kami. Gods are kami. So are some monsters and animals. Even trees and rocks can be kami. People who practice Shinto honor kami with art, festivals, and **shrines**.

Ebisu is one of Japan's most celebrated kami. He is one of the Seven Lucky Gods. For hundreds of years, people around the world have shared Ebisu's story.

Primary Source

Masato Ogata is a Japanese fisher. He explains Ebisu's importance:

> Ebisu is the most important god among fisher folk. We offer him [a drink] without fail each day. . . . When you begin building a boat, when you let out a new net for the first time, when you start a new fishing season, you pray to Ebisu.

Source: Shoko Yoneyama. *Animism in Contemporary Japan*. Taylor & Francis, 2018, p. 56.

What's the Big Idea?

Read this quote carefully. What is its main idea? How is the main idea supported by details?

In Japan, Ebisu is the most well-known member of the *shichifukujin*.

CHAPTER **2**

The Seven Lucky Gods

Japan has seven gods of good luck. They are collectively known as the *shichifukujin* (shee-chee-foo-koo-jeen), or "Seven Lucky Gods." These gods are said to bring joy and good fortune. Each god has a special role.

Jurōjin stands for long life. Daikoku protects farmers. Hotei is the god of happiness. Benten stands for music, literature, and the female spirit. Fukurokuju stands for wisdom. Bishamon protects people from evil.

Ebisu is one of the gods of good luck. He is especially important to fishers and people who own businesses. He also protects the sea.

Most of the *shichifukujin* come from Hindu and Chinese stories. Only Ebisu is **indigenous** to Japan. This is one of the reasons he is so popular among Japanese people.

New Year's Eve

According to popular legend, the Seven Lucky Gods gather together on New Year's Eve.

Seven Lucky Gods

Jurōjin

Daikoku

Hotei

Benten

Fukurokuju

Bishamon

Ebisu

Each of Japan's lucky gods has a unique story, personality, and role.

15

According to legend, the *Takarabune* carries food, gems, and magical objects.

They board a boat called the *Takarabune* (tah-kah-rah-boo-neh), or a "treasure boat." The gods travel across Japan and bring good luck to people in the new year. They also bring presents to children.

People in Japan often spend New Year's Eve preparing for the arrival of the Seven Lucky Gods. Some people travel to seven different shrines, each one dedicated to a different lucky god. They get a stamp at each shrine. Each stamp is placed in a book called a *goshuincho*. People believe that those who collect all seven stamps will have a good year.

Daikoku and Ebisu

In some stories, Ebisu is not the son of Izanagi and Izanami. Instead, he is the son of Daikoku. This may be why Daikoku and Ebisu are often shown together in art. They are also shown together because both gods are connected to food. Today, the two gods are said to protect Japan's wealth.

Mount Fuji is the tallest mountain in Japan. The mountain is a symbol of good luck.

Many people place pictures of the lucky gods under their pillows on New Year's Eve. Anyone who has good dreams containing Mount Fuji, a hawk, or an eggplant will have a lucky year. Those who have bad dreams must place the picture in a stream and let it float away. This carries away any bad luck.

Explore Online

Visit the website below. Does it give any new information about Japanese New Year's Eve traditions that wasn't in Chapter Two?

New Year's Eve in Japan

abdocorelibrary.com/ebisu

Some Japanese fishers pray to Ebisu before starting their day's work.

CHAPTER 3

Honoring Ebisu

Today, Ebisu is a popular god in Japan. Many people worship him. Fishers pray to Ebisu to protect them at sea. They also ask the god to bring them fish.

Many business owners also worship Ebisu. They pray to the god for good fortune.

Their stores often have artwork or statues of Ebisu. This is said to bring good luck.

Ebisu is honored throughout Japan. His statues are seen in public squares. Streets, bridges, and buildings are named after Ebisu. There are also many shrines dedicated to the god. Most are near the coast, where fishers pray for a good catch. The most important one is the Nishinomiya Shrine.

Festivals

Every year, Ebisu is honored with festivals. In early January, big cities such as Kyoto and Osaka hold a celebration for the god. The festival is called Tōka Ebisu. It lasts up to five days. During the celebration, people gather

During Tōka Ebisu, more than 1 million people travel to the Nishinomiya Shrine.

at Ebisu shrines. They pray for wealth and good fortune in the new year. They drop coins in donation boxes. Colorful street stalls sell good luck charms on bamboo branches.

Ebisu is celebrated during October too. Japanese myths call October the Month without Gods. During this month, all the gods leave their shrines to go to the Grand Shrine at Izumo. But because Ebisu is deaf, he does not hear the call to go. He is the only god to stay behind. He stays near the Japanese people to protect them and bring them good luck.

Waking Up Ebisu

At Ebisu festivals, worshippers must let the deaf god know they are praying to him. They knock on a wooden board near his altar to wake him up so he can listen to their prayers. During shrine ceremonies, people clap their hands to wake up the god.

Ebisukō is celebrated with colorful fireworks.

Japanese people celebrate Ebisu as thanks for staying near them. On October 19 and 20, people in Japan hold a festival called Ebisukō. They gather at shrines to pray for wealth. They also buy good luck charms. Merchants set up stalls that sell fish and produce. Many offer discounts to customers.

There are hundreds of Ebisu statues in Japan.

Ebisu in Art

Ebisu is a popular figure in art. He usually has a large head and a short body. He has a beard and a big belly. The god is often shown smiling. In many artworks, Ebisu carries a fishing hook in one hand and a fish in the other. This fish is often a sea bream, a good luck symbol in Japan.

Paintings, woodblock prints, and carved sculptures show Ebisu. His face is placed on coins and good luck charms. He is also shown in plays and puppet shows.

Ebisu is an important god for many Japanese people. He protects people and brings good luck. Hundreds of years after his story was first told, he still fills people with the spirit of joy, luck, and generosity.

Further Evidence

Look at the website below. Does it give new evidence to support Chapter Three?

Ebisu

abdocorelibrary.com/ebisu

Legendary Facts

Hiruko was born without bones. After he was cast away, he took the name Ebisu.

Ebisu is the god of fishers and one of Japan's Seven Lucky Gods.

Each New Year's Eve, Japan celebrates the Seven Lucky Gods.

Ebisu is honored with art, shrines, and festivals.

29

Glossary

disabilities
conditions that make it more difficult for a person to do everyday activities

incarnations
people, animals, or objects that contain the spirit of a god

indigenous
native to a particular place

leech
a freshwater, bloodsucking worm with a flattened body

merchants
business owners

ritual
a series of actions carried out in a specific way, often related to a religious ceremony

shrine
a place where gods and other religious figures are honored and worshipped

Online Resources

To learn more about Ebisu and Japanese mythology, visit our free resource websites below.

Core Library CONNECTION
FREE! COMMON CORE MULTIMEDIA RESOURCES

Visit **abdocorelibrary.com** or scan this QR code for free Common Core resources for teachers and students, including vetted activities, multimedia, and booklinks, for deeper subject comprehension.

Booklinks NONFICTION NETWORK
FREE! ONLINE NONFICTION RESOURCES

Visit **abdobooklinks.com** or scan this QR code for free additional online weblinks for further learning. These links are routinely monitored and updated to provide the most current information available.

Learn More

Fox, Jay. *My First Book of Japanese*. Bushel & Peck, 2022.

Van, R. L. *Japan*. Abdo, 2023.

Yasuda, Yuri. *Japanese Myths, Legends, and Folktales: Bilingual English and Japanese Edition*. Tuttle, 2019.

Index

Ainu, 6
Asia, 9

Ebisukō, 25

goshuincho, 17
Grand Shrine at Izumo, 24

Izanagi, 5–6, 17
Izanami, 5–6, 17

Kyoto, 22

New Year's Eve, 14, 16–19
Nishinomiya Shrine, 22

Osaka, 22

Saburo, Ebisu, 6
Seven Lucky Gods, 10, 13–14, 15, 16–19
Shinto, 9–10

Takarabune, 16
Tōka Ebisu, 22–23

About the Author

Golriz Golkar has written more than 100 nonfiction and fiction books for children. She holds a BA in American literature and culture from UCLA and an EdM in language and literacy from the Harvard Graduate School of Education. She loves to write the kinds of books that students are excited to read.